Fact Finders®

WHAT WENT WRONG?

The Johnstown Flood

CORE EVENTS OF A DEADLY DISASTER

by Marlee Richards

Consultant:
Richard Burkert
President and CEO
Johnstown Area Heritage Association
Johnstown, Pennsylvania

CAPSTONE PRESS
a capstone imprint

Fact Finders Books are published by Capstone Press,
1710 Roe Crest Drive, North Mankato, Minnesota 56003
www.capstonepub.com

Library of Congress Cataloging-in-Publication Data
Richards, Marlee.
  The Johnstown Flood : core events of a deadly disaster / by Marlee Richards.
     pages cm. — (Fact finders. What went wrong?)
  Summary: "Explains the Johnstown Flood, including its chronology, causes, and lasting effects"—
Provided by publisher.
  Includes bibliographical references and index.
  ISBN 978-1-4765-4182-2 (library binding)
  ISBN 978-1-4765-5131-9 (paperback)
  ISBN 978-1-4765-5980-3 (eBook PDF)
1. Floods—Pennsylvania—Johnstown—History—19th century—Juvenile literature. 2. Johnstown
(Pa.)—History—19th century—Juvenile literature. I. Title.
  F159.J7B75 2014
  974.8'77—dc23   2013024122

Editorial Credits
Jennifer Huston, editor; Bobbie Nuytten, designer; Wanda Winch, media researcher; Kathy McColley,
production specialist

Photo Credits
AP Images, 27 (bottom), David J. Phillip, 29; Capstone, 13 (top); Corbis: Royalty-Free, 21; Courtesy
of Johnstown Area Heritage Association, 5, 6, 9, 19, 22, 24, 25, 27 (top); Getty Images Inc: Stock
Montage, 4; Library of Congress: Prints and Photographs Division, cover (all), 8, 14, 16, 18, 23;
National Park Service: artist L. Kenneth Townsend, 11, 13 (b); NOAA: Commander Mark Moran, 28;
Shutterstock: Dr. Morley Read, 1, 7 (right), 15 (b), 20–21 (b), Transia Design, wave design; Wikipedia,
15 (t)

Primary source bibliography
Page 4—*The World* (New York), "Johnstown Blotted Out by the Flood." June 2, 1889.
Page 11—*Baltimore American*, "Warnings Not Heeded." June 2, 1889.
Page 17—*Chicago Daily Tribune*, "Some Hairbreadth Escapes." June 8, 1889.

Printed in the United States of America in North Mankato, Minnesota.
42014   008194R

Table of Contents

CHAPTER 1

Never-Ending Rain

FRANK LESLIE'S

JOHNSTOWN

NEWSPAPER

NEW YORK—FOR THE WEEK ENDING JUNE 8, 1889.

[Price, 10 Cents.

"Johnstown Blotted Out by the Flood!" blared a June 2, 1889, headline in *The World*, a New York City newspaper. The article told of floodwaters raging through Johnstown, a steel mill town in southwestern Pennsylvania. Other papers called the storm that leveled the town the worst flood of the century. More people died as a result of the Johnstown flood than any natural **disaster** in the United States before it. But was this horrible tragedy simply a natural disaster, or did so many lose their lives due to human carelessness?

disaster—an event that causes great damage, loss, or suffering

By the 1880s, residents of Johnstown were used to the rivers flooding frequently. They used clever methods to deal with the inconvenience.

Frequent Flooding

Johnstown is located in a valley in the Allegheny Mountains. There the Little Conemaugh and Stony Creek Rivers join together to form the Conemaugh River. These two rivers drain a steep and mountainous area. This drainage caused Johnstown to frequently flood. Rising rivers and flooding often forced townspeople to move their belongings to higher, drier floors. As a result, the big rainfall at the end of May 1889 seemed typical. Everyone believed the water levels would go down, and they could move their belongings back again. But any more rain would cause great danger to businesses, people, and homes.

Boomtown

Despite the frequent flooding, Johnstown's location proved perfect for industry. Businesses flocked to the community because of its waterways and rich **natural resources**. The mountains nearby held large supplies of limestone, iron, and coal. These **minerals** lay beneath dense pine forests that provided cheap lumber. Giant iron and steel corporations sent steel to Pittsburgh and nationwide from the Conemaugh Valley. Companies and their owners prospered.

Homes and other buildings in Johnstown were constructed at the edge of the riverbank, which frequently flooded.

The largest business in Johnstown was the Cambria Iron Company. Cambria's owners built hundreds of homes so their employees could live near work. But in doing so, builders stripped the nearby mountains of timber that **absorbed** floodwaters. Building homes so close to the river narrowed the riverbed, which meant that the water had to fit into a smaller space. This only added to Johnstown's flooding problems.

natural resource—a material found in nature that is useful to people

mineral—a material found in nature that is not an animal or a plant

absorb—to soak up

A Change of Hands

In 1853 the South Fork Dam and human-made Lake Conemaugh were completed. They were about 14 miles (22.5 kilometers) from Johnstown in the nearby mountains. The dam was 72 feet (22 meters) tall and 931 feet (284 m) long. But by 1889 the clay dam was badly in need of repairs. The dam's owners had done little to maintain it, and it often leaked. They patched the leaks with mud and straw. They also lowered the top of the dam by a few feet, which made it easier for carriages to get across. They even removed the drainage pipes and sold them for scrap.

The South Fork Fishing and Hunting Club bought the dam in 1879. The members were rich Pittsburgh businessmen, including Andrew Carnegie and Andrew Mellon, who built vacation homes in the valley. They made some changes, such as placing a screen across the dam. They fished for sport and wanted to keep fish from swimming downstream. But over time, the screen started collecting trash, which blocked the water's gentle flow.

Andrew Carnegie made a fortune in the steel industry. He also gave a lot of his money to charity.

This picture shows a man canoeing on Lake Conemaugh. Fish screens can be seen along the bottom of the photo.

Lake Conemaugh was about two miles (3.2 km) long and 1 mile (1.6 km) wide at its widest spot. It covered an area of about 320 football fields!

A Surprising Turn of Events

Trouble first began on Thursday, May 30, 1889. At first, the rain trickled down. But after some heavy downpours, the area was completely soaked. The heavy rains continued throughout the night and all day on Friday.

By morning the Conemaugh and Stony Creek rivers **crested** high at their banks. Soon there was 3 to 10 feet (about 1 to 3 meters) of water in the streets. Families rushed to higher floors as water rose higher inside their homes. Many people feared that the South Fork Dam might break.

crest—to reach the highest point

"We were afraid of that lake ... No one could see the immense height to which that ... dam had been built without fearing the tremendous power of the water behind it ... "

—*A longtime Johnstown resident as quoted in the* Baltimore American, *June 2, 1889*

This painting shows a peaceful Lake Conemaugh and the South Fork Dam before it burst. Carriages would often travel along the top of the dam.

CHAPTER 2

Trouble at the South Fork Dam:
May 31, 1889

The townspeople knew about the dam's problems for years, but most residents ignored the warning signs. That's exactly what happened when a **telegraph** operator sent warning to Johnstown—no one paid attention.

During that terrible storm, telegraph operators throughout the Conemaugh Valley sent messages about possible trouble. Several smaller rivers fed the upper part of Lake Conemaugh, and they were all overflowing. Colonel Elias Unger, president of the South Fork Fishing and Hunting Club, quickly had a ditch dug around the dam. This was done so that the excess water had a place to go, but water soon overflowed the ditch. So Unger sent a man on horseback to urge the residents of nearby towns to **evacuate**.

The Dam Burst

Around 3:10 p.m. on May 31, the worst happened. A sheet of water 300 feet (91.4 m) wide poured over the dam. The rushing water cut a hole through the dam's center. Within minutes, 20 million tons (18 million metric tons) of water exploded from the dam. The force was equal to water gushing over Niagara Falls for 36 minutes.

FLOOD FACT

After the dam burst, Lake Conemaugh was completely drained of water in about 45 minutes.

telegraph—a machine that uses electronic signals to send messages over long distances

evacuate—to leave an area during a time of danger

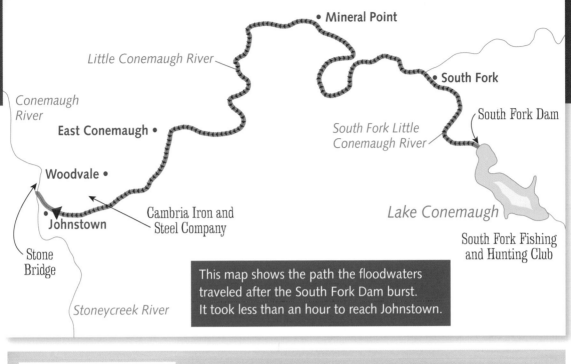

• **Mineral Point**

Little Conemaugh River

Conemaugh River

East Conemaugh •

• **South Fork**

South Fork Dam

South Fork Little Conemaugh River

Woodvale •

Cambria Iron and Steel Company

Lake Conemaugh

• **Johnstown**

Stone Bridge

South Fork Fishing and Hunting Club

Stoneycreek River

This map shows the path the floodwaters traveled after the South Fork Dam burst. It took less than an hour to reach Johnstown.

This painting shows what it looked like when the South Fork Dam broke, and all the water in Lake Conemaugh was set free.

As the wave of water thundered down the mountain and into the valley, it picked up size and speed. Eventually, the wave reached 40 feet (12.2 m) high—the height of a four-story building. As the wall of water raced through the valley, it destroyed everything in its path—buildings, trees, animals, and people. One by one, entire towns were flattened.

The giant wave hit Johnstown at 40 miles (64 km) per hour. The gushing water broke wooden houses into pieces like twigs. One house was torn apart by a floating railcar. Many people had sought safety on roofs and hung on for dear life. But roofs were ripped from buildings and simply floated away. Flying **debris** crushed many people who had escaped drowning. Floodwaters flung a 170,000-pound (77,111-kilogram) train almost a mile.

The warehouse of the Cambria Iron Company (background) was destroyed by the flood. A railcar rests on its side in the foreground.

A couple miles east of Johnstown, people who were on a train in East Conemaugh faced a similar horror. As water rushed through the rail yard, trains toppled and were swept away like they were toys. Passengers and crew members fled to higher ground or hung on to floating rubble. Others faced a watery grave.

Onlookers watched the horrific scene as homes, buildings, friends, and neighbors were swept away by the raging water.

A WARNING SIGNAL

Engineer John Hess was sitting in his train at the Conemaugh rail yards when he heard the flood coming his way. He quickly drove his train west, with the whistle sounding the whole time. This signal warned people all around of the danger. Just before the swell of floodwater hit Hess' train, he jumped off and ran to higher ground. His warning saved many lives, and he was later honored for his bravery.

debris—the scattered pieces of something that has been broken or destroyed; garbage

15

Stone Bridge Pileup

Only the Stone Bridge held firm. It spanned the Conemaugh River on the edge of Johnstown. The bridge partly blocked the rush of water, but that caused a backup of trash, trees, and trapped humans and animals. The result was a **whirlpool** of rushing water that swirled everything in it for 10 minutes. Trapped **survivors** clung to anything they could find to keep their heads above water.

whirlpool—a water current that moves rapidly in a circle

survivor—someone who lives through a disaster or horrible event

A pile of wood from downed trees, broken homes, and other debris quickly formed near the bridge. Onlookers watched in horror when it burst into flames and ignited the bridge. No one knows for sure how the fire started. But hundreds of people on the bridge were forced to choose between burning to death or drowning in the whirlpool below.

After the flood caused a pileup of debris at the Stone Bridge, a fire started, which lasted for days.

TALE OF TERROR

"A young hero sat upon the roof of his ... house holding his mother and little sister ... [T]he boy sprang into one of the windows. As he turned to rescue his mother and sister, the house swung out ... and the boy, seeing that there was no possibility of getting them off, leaped back to their side. A second time the house was stopped, this time by a tree. The boy helped his mother and sister to a place of safety in the tree; but before he could leave the roof, the house was swept on and he was drowned."

—"Some Hairbreadth Escapes,"
Chicago Daily Tribune,
June 8, 1889.

Surviving Johnstown

The raging waters of the flood quickly passed, but the **fiery** blaze lasted three days. After it was over, survivors searched for loved ones. The dead were lined up on schoolhouse desks or on church pews. Survivors faced a grim sight.

fiery—marked by fire

A man poses on top of a railroad car in front of a house that was destroyed in the flood.

People used whatever they could find to build temporary shelters like this one, even debris from the flood.

In the end, 2,209 people died in the flood, including 750 bodies that were never claimed. Ninety-nine families were completely wiped out.

The search for bodies went on for weeks. The smell of death was everywhere. Everyone looked for loved ones and traces of their belongings but without much success.

More than 1,600 homes were destroyed. Many more were damaged and too dangerous for living. The flood caused $17 million in damage. That was at a time when the average person made only $10 per week.

Rescue Efforts

Just a day after the flood, food and relief supplies arrived from Pittsburgh. Soon help arrived from across the country and around the world. Doctors came to tend to the injured. The **American Red Cross** set up places for thousands of homeless people to receive food and shelter. Even inmates from a Pittsburgh prison helped out by baking loaves of bread for the people of Johnstown. Thousands of people came from across the country to help restore train service, build new bridges, and remove debris.

Reporters also flocked to the valley. They sent daily reports to eager readers. As a result of this attention, more than $3.7 million in donations poured in from around the world. The money was used to rebuild the city and help out those who had lost loved ones in the flood.

> **American Red Cross**—an organization started by Clara Barton to respond when a disaster occurs

Johnstown Flood Timeline

1839: Construction begins on South Fork Dam to contain the water from Lake Conemaugh.

1852: Cambria Iron Company of Johnstown founded.

1853: South Fork Dam completed.

1854: Johnstown becomes a stop on the main line of the Pennsylvania Railroad and is connected with the Baltimore and Ohio Railroad.

1858: Cambria Iron Company of Johnstown becomes a leading producer of steel rails in the United States.

1879: South Fork Fishing and Hunting Club buys and makes changes to the dam.

1839 . . . .

CLARA BARTON TO THE RESCUE

Teacher and nurse Clara Barton established the American Red Cross in 1881. She wanted to start an organization that would supply aid after natural disasters. Within days after the 1889 flood, Barton arrived in Johnstown. It was her group's first major relief effort. She brought in 50 doctors and nurses and ordered the construction of six large buildings. One held supplies, food, clothing, and building materials sent from other states. The other "Red Cross Hotels" sheltered the homeless. Barton stayed in Johnstown for nearly five months.

1881: Engineer John Fulton inspects the dam and reports critical areas in need of repair.

1888: Herbert Webber, an employee at the club, reports leaks in the dam.

1889 May 30–31: Heavy rains cover the Conemaugh Valley.

1889 May 31, 1:00 p.m.: Water starts to spill over the top of the South Fork Dam.

1889 May 31, 3:10 p.m.: South Fork Dam breaks.

1889 May 31, 4:07 p.m.: A wall of water hits Johnstown, flooding the city.

1880

1890

CHAPTER 3
Solving Johnstown's Flooding Problems

As relief efforts took hold, questions loomed about how this horrific disaster could have happened. Who was to blame?

City leaders considered the building of so many new homes along the riverbank and the resulting loss of trees. But their main focus was on the dam. Club members wanted everyone to believe that the dam broke because of natural causes. But many townspeople thought the dam should have been repaired years earlier. It continued to leak frequently. In 1881 engineer John Fulton reported that the dam was badly in need of repairs.

This empty lake bed is where the 72-foot- (22 m-) tall South Fork Dam used to be.

El. of Breast of Dam +1618.'

72 Ft.

Andrew Carnegie built a library in Johnstown after the flood.

Lawsuits were filed against club members, including leading businessmen Andrew Carnegie and Henry Frick. They were charged with neglect of the dam. But the courts sided with the club members, saying that an "act of God" caused the dam to break. The club members were never required to pay a penny in damages. Without a win in court, survivors had no legal way to collect on their losses.

Some club members donated to relief programs and helped rebuild the city. Carnegie contributed $10,000 to relief programs. He also built a library that currently houses the Johnstown Flood Museum.

Steel mills were up and running within a month after the flood. Some stores reopened by July. Those who were able to go back to work did. Some people moved away, but most simply started over.

Within five years, the city looked as if the "flood of the century" had never happened. Within 20 years, Johnstown's population had doubled, and the city was producing four times as much steel as in 1889.

This family sold coffee and sandwiches to flood survivors.

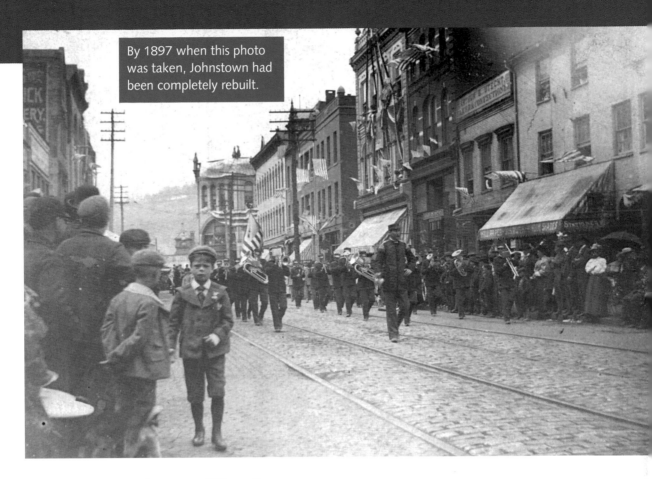

By 1897 when this photo was taken, Johnstown had been completely rebuilt.

Preventing Future Floods

Even after the city was rebuilt, Johnstown still had flooding problems. Solutions needed to be put in place to prevent future disasters, so Johnstown banned the dumping of garbage in the river. This ban resulted in greater flow of water. With less debris to raise water levels, they stayed lower.

Officials also limited building along riverbanks to widen pathways for water flow. And they ordered new flood walls built, this time out of brick, stone, or concrete. No one wanted the new walls to leak the way the clay South Fork Dam did.

CHAPTER 4
Comparing the Johnstown Flood to Other Floods

Even with these changes, Johnstown suffered from other terrible floods. Three days of rain and melting snow caused another major flood in 1936. This flood caused 24 deaths and $41 million in damage. It also destroyed 77 buildings and damaged 3,000 others.

As a result, the federal government passed the Flood Control Act of 1936. This law allowed the **Army Corps of Engineers** to plan flood-control projects wherever they were needed. That included the Johnstown Local Flood Protection Program in 1943. With this program, several improvements were made, including increasing the amount of water the rivers could hold. Meanwhile, the state government passed a special tax to cover the costs of future flood recovery needs.

These improvements prevented another major flood in Johnstown until 1977. In mid-July of that year, severe thunderstorms dropped about 12 inches (30 centimeters) of rain, which caused flooding. Even with the flood controls in place, the 1977 flood resulted in 85 deaths and $300 million in damage. As in the 1889 flood, investigators blamed several dams that failed to hold back water. Once again, more planning and better engineering were needed to prevent further flooding.

Improvements like flood walls made the river wider and deeper, which helped control future flooding.

Despite the flood controls that had been put in place, another major flood occurred in Johnstown in 1977.

Army Corps of Engineers—a U.S. agency that works on outdoor projects, including flood protection and building canals and dams

FLOOD FACT

Lake Conemaugh no longer exists. Part of the town of St. Michael sits on what used to be Lake Conemaugh.

An Ongoing Process

Recent history shows that flood control is an ongoing process. In August 2005, Hurricane Katrina swept through the South, destroying towns on the coasts of Mississippi, Alabama, and Louisiana. However, it was the flooding that followed the hurricane that caused the most damage.

Similar to the dam breaking in Johnstown, the **levees**, or protective dams, broke in New Orleans, Louisiana. In both cases this caused major flooding.

When the levees broke in New Orleans, the city was left under several feet of water.

levee—a bank built up near a river to prevent flooding

28

Officials were unprepared for the flooding in New Orleans in 2005. Some residents were forced to wait on their roofs for help for several days.

In New Orleans, 53 levees overflowed, flooding about 80 percent of the city. People flocked to the roofs of tall buildings and the city's football stadium—the Superdome—for protection. But the city, state, and federal governments were terribly unprepared, and relief efforts were significantly delayed. In the end, 1,836 people died. Katrina was one of the costliest natural disasters in U.S. history, with damages reaching $81.2 billion.

But the 1889 Johnstown flood remains in history books as the disaster that shocked the world. The loss of lives and the amount of destruction were a wake-up call to the town and the entire nation.

FLOOD FACT

The National Park Service currently runs the Johnstown Flood National Memorial. It is located on the site where part of Lake Conemaugh, the South Fork Dam, and the clubhouse used to stand.

Glossary

absorb (ab-ZORB)—to soak up

American Red Cross (uh-MER-un-kuhn RED KRAWSS)—an organization started by Clara Barton to respond when a disaster occurs

Army Corps of Engineers (AR-mee KOR uhv en-juh-NEERZ)—a U.S. agency that works on outdoor projects, including flood protection and building canals and dams

crest (KREST)—to reach the highest point

debris (duh-BREE)—the scattered pieces of something that has been broken or destroyed; garbage

disaster (di-ZAS-tuhr)—an event that causes great damage, loss, or suffering

evacuate (i-VA-kyuh-wayt)—to leave an area during a time of danger

fiery (FIRE-ee)—marked by fire

levee (LEV-ee)—a bank built up near a river to prevent flooding

mineral (MIN-ur-uhl)—a material found in nature that is not an animal or a plant

natural resource (NACH-ur-uhl REE-sorss)—a material found in nature that is useful to people

survivor (sur-VIVE-or)—someone who lives through a disaster or horrible event

telegraph (TEL-uh-graf)—a machine that uses electronic signals to send messages over long distances

whirlpool (WURL-pool)—a water current that moves rapidly in a circle

Internet Sites

FactHound offers a safe, fun way to find Internet sites related to this book. All of the sites on FactHound have been researched by our staff.

Here's all you do:

Visit *www.facthound.com*

Type in this code: 9781476541822

Super-cool stuff! Check out projects, games and lots more at **www.capstonekids.com**

Critical Thinking Using the Common Core

1. Do you think the Johnstown flood was caused by nature, human carelessness, or a combination of both factors? Support your answer with details from the text. (Key Ideas and Details)

2. Look at the timeline on pages 20–21. How long did it take for the city to build up to flood conditions? How long did it take for rescue forces to get to Johnstown and repair the damage? Compare and discuss the amount of time for each event. (Craft and Structure)

3. How well do you think cities and states are prepared for floods today? Support your answer with facts from the text as well as from research from print and online sources. (Integration of Knowledge and Ideas)

Read More

Dougherty, Terri. *The Worst Floods of All Time*. Edge Books: Epic Disasters. North Mankato, Minn.: Capstone Press, 2013.

Dunn, Joeming. *Clara Barton*. Graphic Planet: Bio-Graphics. Edina, Minn.: Magic Wagon, 2009.

Mullins, Matt. *How Did They Build That? Dam*. Community Connections. Ann Arbor, Mich.: Cherry Lake Publishing, 2010.

Woods, Michael, and Mary B. Woods. *Floods*. Disasters Up Close. Minneapolis: Lerner Publications Company, 2007.

Index